What God Is, *Only* God Is

Sylvia Burnett

C.I.Y. Publishing
P.O. Box 1822
Fallbrook, CA 92088
www.christinyou.net

WHAT GOD IS, ONLY GOD IS

Sylvia Burnett

Published by
C.I.Y. Publishing
P.O. Box 1822
Fallbrook, CA 92088-1822

ISBN 978-1-929541-56-0

Printed in the United States of America

Introduction

"What God is, *only* God is." That's one of two premises put forth by contemporary Christian theologian James A. Fowler (1946-20__) in his article entitled "Towards a Christian Understanding of God" (available for download at Jim's website: www.Christinyou.com).

The many articles and books written by Jim (my older brother) reveal unique insights about God; but Jim's works are so deep and heavy—filled with such complex theological concepts and big words—that most Christians would need the aid of a theological dictionary to wade through them. (Even our own mother, when reading Jim's works, complained that he used too many big words, making it difficult for the average Christian to understand.)

I have written this book specifically for the average Christian reader. It presents a "lighter" look at the subject of "a Christian understanding of God" ... purposely avoiding the big words and deep theological complexities used by Jim. Using the Bible as the definitive authority on the subject of God, this study examines the multi-faceted character of God, considering His attributes one by one.

The short chapters make this book ideal for use as a personal daily devotional reader. It would also be suitable for use by a Bible study group desiring to know God better. While writing it, I came to know Him better ... and was delighted to find that I loved Him more! Having been a Christian for over fifty years, I was somewhat surprised by this, and most definitely pleased. Truly, I have been blest by this undertaking.

Exploring the query posed in Psalm 113:5, "Who is like the Lord our God?", this book affirms that "there is none like God" (Deut. 33:26). "What God is, *only* God is."

Sylvia Burnett
Nov 2015

Sincere thanks to my brother Jim for permission to use his ideas/words in this book, and for his assistance in getting it published. — SB

Chapter 1

GOD IS

SELF-

EXISTENT

"What God is, *only* God is."

God is Self-existent; *only* God is Self-existent.

The Bible makes no attempt to prove that God exists. It simply accepts His existence as fact, and proceeds with the story: "In the beginning God created ... " (Gen. 1:1).

"There are fools who say in their hearts, 'There is no God'." They are corrupt, they commit evil acts ... they have no understanding, those evildoers ... and do not call upon God (Ps. 53:1,4). But all the wondrous things on and in the Earth, along with the beauty and mystery of the heavens, attest to the fact that God exists.

For centuries Christian theologians have discussed the question of who, or what, caused God to come into existence. Is there some obscure reference about that subject in the Bible? It seems

1

not. The Bible doesn't even hint at the possibility that there was any force or power—nothing, no one, no event, no catastrophic explosion, etc.—that brought about the existence of God. Nor does the Bible suggest that God was created, or even that He created Himself.

There is no evidence at all that God was caused or created by any person or event outside Himself ... which leaves only one conclusion: God exists in and of Himself. He Himself is the very essence of existence. He *is* Self-existent.

What is He like, this Self-existent God? What is His character? Simply put, God is the epitome of all that is good, and His attributes manifest all that is good: He is pure, holy, righteous, faithful, etc.

Because of His unique existence and character, there is none other "like God."

Chapter 2

GOD IS

CREATOR

"What God is, *only* God is."

God is Creator; *only* God is Creator.

The Bible does not explain *why* God began creating, but it does declare repeatedly that He created everything that exists. All that exists (apart from God Himself) was created by God. The recorded history of God's creative work begins: "In the beginning God created ... " (Gen. 1:1).

Neither does the Bible include a record of the creation of Heaven and the wonders that exist there, but we know that God created it all: the throne upon which He sits, the river of life, the streets of pure gold, the various heavenly beings— cherubim, seraphim, angels, fantastic winged creatures full of eyes inside and out, etc. God had a purpose for creating each heavenly being, and to each He assigned a specific task.

God's perfect peace pervaded Heaven until the angel Lucifer became dissatisfied with his humble role as servant, stirred up trouble, and was

3

cast out of Heaven (Isa. 14:12ff). (A more detailed account of this event is given in a later chapter entitled "God is good.")

The Biblical account of God's creation begins with His creation of the heavens, the vast universe with its many galaxies filled with stars and planets. On one of those planets (the Earth, on which we live) God created an appropriate habitation for mankind (Isa. 45:18), complete with dry land and seas and rivers, mountains and valleys and deserts and jungles, air suitable for man to breathe, etc.

The Bible records creation as a 7-day process. (Geological studies have revealed that the duration of each day was much longer than the 24-hour period we now call a day.) Six days God created, and at the end of each day He declared it good, and on the 7th day He rested. Not that He was tired, for God never grows weary (Isa. 40:28). Perhaps He simply wanted to survey and contemplate all that He had done—for it was, indeed, quite wonderful!

God used His extraordinary imagination to create all that exists, including mankind, which He created "in His image" (Gen. 1:26-27). All of God's creation displays the perfection, purpose, and plan He had in mind—that He Himself should be glorified (Ps. 86:8-10). He created all things for His own glory (Isa. 43:7).

"God is Creator, *only* God is Creator."

4

Chapter 3

GOD IS

ONE

"What God is, *only* God is."

God is One; *only* God is One.

The Christian understanding of God is unique,
differing from all other concepts of God. It is
probably most similar to that the Jewish faith, from
which the Christian faith emerged, with Abraham as
their earliest patriarch. Both the Christians and the
Jews believe in the one true God, and that He is
superior to the various "other gods" worshipped
around the world.

      Christians, however, believe the one true
God is a Triune God, comprised of three Persons in
one Being (one God). This three-Person Godhead
is sometimes referred to as the Trinity. Non-
Christians scoff at the idea, saying that the Christian
God is a freak—a three-headed God. But of course
that is not true.

      Part of the difficulty in understanding the
concept of a Triune God is that we are physical
human beings, trying to comprehend God, Who is

5

Spirit. As physical beings we cannot fully grasp the reality of the spirit world, a world very different than that in which we live. Thus, it is not possible for us to fully understand how God can be three Persons in one Being. But because that is what the Bible reveals, we believe it to be so.

The three Persons of the Trinity are:
– the Father,
– the Son (Who was named Jesus when born as a baby in Bethlehem— Luke 1:31; Matt. 1:21,25), and
– the Holy Spirit.

As they are united in one Being, they are united in purpose; they act together to accomplish the perfect Will of God.

There are times when one Person of the Trinity engages in a distinct function. For example, it was the Son Who took on the "God incarnate" mission—coming to Earth and being "born" as a physical human being, going about doing good and glorifying God, enduring an excruciatingly painful death by crucifixion, being raised from the dead and finally being received back into Heaven. It is important to note, however, that the Son remained unified in the one Being of God while engaged in this distinct function.

Another example: It was the Holy Spirit Who caused Mary to become pregnant with Jesus

(Matt. 1:18-20). And after Jesus was baptized by John the Baptist, it was the Holy Spirit Who descended from Heaven in the visible form of a dove to attest to the purity of Jesus (Luke 3:22). Again it must be noted that while performing these specific tasks, the Holy Spirit remained unified in the one Being of God.

Always, the three Persons of the Trinity remain unified as One. God *is* One.

The mind-boggling concept of a multi-Person Godhead was introduced by Jesus one day when He was in the temple in Jerusalem with His disciples. With the Jews gathered around, Jesus said, "I and the Father are one" (John 10:30). That radical statement, which the Jewish leaders declared to be blasphemous, intimated that God is a plural Being—comprised of more than one Person. It was a totally new concept about the Oneness of God, and completely unacceptable to the Jews.

Later, when Jesus was alone with His disciples, He spoke of the third Person of the Godhead, the Holy Spirit.
"I will ask the Father, and He will give you another Helper to be with you forever" (John 14:16-17)—the Helper, "the Spirit of truth" (John 15:26).
"When the Spirit of truth comes, He will guide you into all the truth" (John 16:13); He "will teach you everything, and remind you of all that I have said to you" (John 14:26).

To Christians the premise that "God is One; *only* God is One" actually means: "God is Trinitarian One; *only* God is Trinitarian One"— three Persons in one Being. Since we cannot fully (intellectually) understand that concept, it is by faith alone that we believe in a Triune God—and by doing so we set ourselves apart from the rest of the world.

Chapter 4

GOD IS

GOOD

"What God is, *only* God is."

God is good; *only* God is good.

Jesus Himself, during His brief teaching ministry
here on Earth, declared that God *is* good. In fact,
He clarified that truth by declaring that *only* God is
good (Luke 18:19). Luke's account of the incident
reports that a rich man came to Jesus and asked,
"Good teacher, what must I do to inherit eternal
life?" Before answering the man's question, Jesus
said to him, "Why do you call Me good? No one is
good except God alone."

In this world it is evident that there are two
opposing forces at work: good and evil. Since God
is good, and all that He created is good, where did
evil come from? Not from God! — so it must have
come from one of God's created beings. (Since
there was a time when only God existed, any thing
or being that is not God Himself was created by
God.)

The story of the origin of evil is revealed in the book of Isaiah (14:12ff): In Heaven the angel Lucifer was dissatisfied with his servant role; he wanted to be worshipped, like the Most High God. (It seems that heavenly beings, created by God to serve and worship Him, have freedom of choice in that regard. They can willingly perform the function God intended for them, or face the consequences of not doing so.) Lucifer's desire to be worshipped like God stirred up trouble and caused turmoil in Heaven.

Because it is imperative that God's heavenly kingdom be free of dissension and discord, reflecting His own perfect peace, Lucifer's rebellious attitude could not be tolerated. God cannot overlook or tolerate anything that is contrary to, or incompatible with, His own perfect nature. To do so would be to "deny Himself," which He cannot do (II Tim: 2:13).

So God cast Lucifer out of Heaven, sending him to Earth where he was allowed to set up his own little kingdom, to be worshipped and served by those angels who had transferred their allegiance from God to Lucifer and departed with him from Heaven.

No longer called Lucifer, on Earth he is known by many names and titles, including Satan, the evil one, the devil, the liar, the deceiver, ruler of this world, prince of darkness, etc.

Satan uses lies and deception to recruit additional subjects to worship and serve him in his earthly kingdom. The encounter between the serpent (Satan) and Eve in the Garden of Eden (Gen. 3) was Satan's first opportunity to entice human beings to honor him instead of God. It is a classic example of Satan's wily ways—which he has continued to use with remarkable success throughout the history of mankind.

There is much evil in this world ruled by Satan. Wickedness abounds! But even so, we should not be overly distressed, for just as God reassured the Old Testament people, He also reassures us today: "My Spirit abides among you; do not fear" (Hag. 2:5).

God *is* good—and He is ultimately in control of all things. The struggle between good and evil will eventually come to an end and a new world order will be established. God has it all planned out. Just wait and watch. It's going to be very exciting!

Chapter 5

GOD IS

IMMORTAL

"What God is, *only* God is."

God is immortal; *only* God is immortal.

Not too long after the end of WW II the rumor
started going 'round that God was dead. That was a
hot topic for several years, especially on college
campuses among students too young to have
experienced the need to depend on God for
protection while serving in the armed forces during
the war.

Those who believed the rumor to be true
were not distressed by it, but rather quite relieved—
as they considered the death of God to be a release
from the standards He had established for proper
conduct, thus allowing them to do whatever they
felt like doing … to use their own desires as the
guideline for acceptable behavior. (Satan must have
been so pleased with himself as he instigated that lie
and saw the results of it.)

But the rumor had no basis of truth in it, for
God cannot die. The Bible says that He *is* immortal

(I Tim. 1:17; 6:16). It's one of the essential attributes of God, that He will never die. The word "immortality" literally means: exemption from death. God will exist forever (Ps. 119:89).

Another way to express this concept might be to say that God *is* life. "He has life in Himself" (John 5:26). He does not derive life from any source outside Himself. He *is* life, in and of Himself, and therefore cannot die. God *is* immortal.

Some Christians believe they will become immortal, "like God," when they get to Heaven, after their physical death here on Earth. But that is true only in the sense that they will "share" God's immortality in His heavenly kingdom. Part of the confusion concerning this matter is brought about by the Apostle Paul's reference to the final days (I Cor. 15:53), when the dead shall be raised and believers shall "put on immortality."

The meaning of the phrase "put on immortality" is: to be enveloped in, or to be clothed in, like a garment. In Heaven, those of us who love Him and are welcomed into His presence shall be clothed in God's immortality.

Human beings can never become immortal—for God is immortal, and "what God is, *only* God is." We cannot become "like God" ... but we can rejoice that when we get to Heaven we shall abide with Him forever, clothed in His immortality and the white robe of righteousness He prepares for us (Rev. 3:4-5).

Chapter 6

GOD IS

LOVE

"What God is, *only* God is."

God is love; *only* God is love.

Love is, first and foremost, relational. For love to exist, there must be at least two persons involved, because love is something you feel for someone else, you share with someone else, you freely give to someone else.

Consider the love relationship among the three Persons Who comprise the Triune God— Father, Son, and Holy Spirit. The Father loves the Son and the Holy Spirit, the Son loves the Father and the Holy Spirit, and the Holy Spirit loves the Father and the Son. They are complete in their love for one another, having no *need* for love from anyone else.

When God created man, He gave him the capacity to love. Now isn't that interesting? There's no indication in the Bible that God gave that ability to any other of His creation: not to the stars and planets in the heavens, not to plants or

animals ... not even to the heavenly beings, if
Lucifer's lack of love for God is a true indicator. It
seems that God gave the capacity to love only to
human beings ... perhaps so they could have a
"relationship" of love with Him? ... so they could
love Him back?

Could this be what God was referring to
when He said (in Genesis 1:26), "Let Us make man
in Our own image." Was He speaking of the
capacity to love? While God did not *need* for
anyone else to love Him (as He is complete in
Himself, having no needs), He *desired* that His
human creatures would do so. Of course, since He
also gave them freedom of choice, they were free to
love Him or not, as they wished, and God knew full
well that not all of them would. But some would!
His heart delights in those who love Him, and
grieves over those who do not.

Human beings are made "in the image of
God" but are not truly "like God." No human being
is love in the same sense that God *is* love, for "what
God is, *only* God is."

Since God *is* love (John 4:16), it's hard to
imagine His hating anyone or anything. But the
Bible tells us that He does (Prov. 6:16-19; Zech.
8:17). What, or who, does God hate? God hates all
that is contrary to His own loving character. For
example, God hates sin (and by extension, Satan,
who lures people into sin); God hates injustice; God
hates a lying witness; God hates a heart that devises

wicked plans; God hates the one who sows discord in a family, etc.

It is important to understand that the love of God is what God *is* in Himself. The Bible does not say that God *has* love—something He can give, distribute, or dispense to His created beings—but rather that God *is* love. The very essence of God is love. The love of God is an integral part of His character, and as such, is not transferable to mankind.

Some people believe that hate is the opposite of love. But in reality the opposite of love is selfishness ... self-orientation rather than other-orientation. The act of loving puts the focus on someone else rather than on self.

A practical guideline for loving others is provided by the Golden Rule: Do unto others as you would have them do unto you (Matt. 7:12). Simply said, loving others means "doing good." According to Acts 10:38, that's what Jesus did while here on Earth: "He went about doing good."

Chapter 7

GOD IS

BEING

"What God is, *only* God is."

God is Being; *only* God is Being.

In its broadest sense, the word "being" has to do
with that which exists. God exists, thus it can
rightly be said that God *is* Being.

    We see around us, however, things that exist
but which we wouldn't define as beings: rocks, for
example, and the stars and planets in the heavens.
A narrower definition is needed. Perhaps a being
could be defined as a living thing. Except that
plants are alive, and we don't think of them as
beings. Then let's narrow our definition even
further, limiting it by using psychological
terminology. It has been stated that beings are living
things with intellectual, volitional, and emotional
capacity (having mind, will, and emotion). In that
sense, only people and animals would be considered
beings (along with the heavenly beings God created
to serve and worship Him in Heaven).

Even by using that much narrower definition, we can still affirm that God *is* Being. And of course we must not forget that there is none "like God"—that all other beings were created by God and are thus lesser beings. "What God is, *only* God is."

In the Old Testament, God identified Himself as "personal" Being: "I AM that I AM" (Exod. 3:14). Jesus, in revealing His divinity while on Earth, used that same "I AM" identification: "Before Abraham was, I AM" (John 8:58), He said; and to the Samaritan woman at the well, Jesus explained, "I AM He (the expected Messiah)" (John 4:26).

Those listening to Jesus speak often found the meaning of His words elusive. Without doubt they had difficulty understanding His meaning when He said, "I and the Father are one" (John 10:30). Jesus was revealing God to be relational Being, saying that more than one Person comprised the one true God—and that He, Jesus, was one of those Persons!

His listeners were incredulous! How could Jesus, a mere physical human being, possibly be one with God, Who *is* divine Spirit? The Jewish leaders were irate; they accused Jesus of blasphemy and wanted to stone Him, but He slipped away (John 10:31-39).

Through Jesus, God revealed Himself as personal and relational Being. "What God is, *only* God is."

Chapter 8

GOD IS

HOLY

"What God is, *only* God is."

God is Holy; *only* God is Holy.

The Bible declares that God *is* Holy ... that God *alone* is Holy (I Sam. 2:2; Rev. 15:4). God defined Himself in that way: "I the Lord your God am Holy" (Lev. 19:2, 20:7).

From His "holy habitation, from Heaven" (Deut. 26:15), "the One Who inhabits eternity" (Isa. 57:15) exhorts mankind to be holy, knowing full well of course that we cannot *be* holy in the way He *is* Holy. God is speaking about holy conduct and holiness of heart (let us not forget that God sees on the heart and knows our every thought and motive).

In the Bible when a person is called holy, it is this attitude of holiness that is being noted. Whenever holy character is exhibited by a human being, it is, in reality, God's holy character being manifested in and through that person. He/She is simply a "channel" through which God expresses

23

His character. Christians are sometimes referred to as "holy ones" or saints, which is an identity derived from the indwelling Spirit. But no one is holy in the same way that God *is* Holy.

And finally we note that God's name is Holy (Isa. 57:15). We are to "glory in His holy name" (I Chron. 16:10) and to "praise His great and awesome name" (Ps. 99:3). One of Christendom's most popular hymns (inspired by Rev. 4:8) expresses this well:

> Holy, Holy, Holy! Lord God Almighty!
> Early in the morning our song shall rise to
>   Thee.
> Holy, Holy, Holy! Merciful and mighty!
> God in three Persons, blessed Trinity.
>
> Holy, Holy, Holy! Though the darkness
>   hide Thee,
> Though the eye of sinful man Thy glory may
>   not see.
> Only Thou art Holy; there is none beside
>   Thee,
> Perfect in power, in love, and purity.

Chapter 9

GOD IS
GRACIOUS

"What God is, *only* God is."

God is gracious; *only* God is gracious.

Repeatedly God dealt graciously with the Old
Testament Jews, being compassionate and merciful
to them.

And what did He expect from them? Love
and obedience: worshipping only Him, the true
God, and keeping His commandments. But they
disappointed Him greatly.

WHY did God act with such compassion
toward people who were obviously not of good
moral character? ... who obviously did not love
Him? Because God *is* gracious (Ps. 103:8),
compassionate, kind, merciful. That is His nature,
so He could not act in any other way. The problem
was, there was a serious shortage of men of good
character— even after the Flood by which God
destroyed all mankind on the Earth except the eight
people on the Ark and started over again (Gen 7:11-
9:18).

From among the men available, God chose
Abram (Gen. 12:1-2) to begin a lineage of godly
men who would honor Him. Through the years this
"chosen people" increased in number, but they
made little progress toward becoming a holy people,
faithful to God. In spite of that fact, through all the
disappointment, God remained gracious and
merciful (true to His own character), providing for
their needs and protecting them (Ps. 111:4; 116:5-
6).

Even today the unchanging God remains
gracious to mankind … and what does God desire
from us? Love and obedience … "love Me and
keep My commandments."

In this world ruled by Satan, there are not
many who love God and acknowledge Him as Lord,
but He knows those of us who do and is gracious to
us, always. How can we show our love and
gratitude to this gracious God? By devoting
ourselves to "good works" (Titus 3:8)—not only to
acts of benevolence and charity in service to others,
but also to a righteous and holy lifestyle that
glorifies God.

May our every word and deed glorify God!

Chapter 10

GOD IS

RIGHTEOUS

"What God is, *only* God is."

God is righteous; *only* God is righteous.

The word "righteous" is defined as being morally upright; just. In God's dealings with mankind, He is just, fair, and always does what is right. As the Old Testament psalmist declared, "... the Lord is upright; He is my rock, and there is no unrighteousness in Him" (Ps. 92:15).

    Only God is righteous; the Bible tells us; "there is no one who is righteous, not even one" (Rom 3:11). We can imitate the righteousness of God, we can try to live a righteous life, but we can never *be* righteous "like God."

.   The psalmist prayed to God, " ... in Your righteousness, give me life" (Ps. 119:40). Indeed there is a direct correlation between righteousness and life. When the Son came to Earth, God revealed His righteousness through the Son. Through faith in Jesus people who are righteous will acquire life (Rom. 1:17).

27

When the inhabitants of a nation are righteous, the result is peace—no internal strife, no conflicts with other nations—and quietness (Isaiah 32:17). Sadly, our nation is not a righteous one. The mass murders that occur all too frequently, the racial tension that erupts in violence, the lack of compassionate care for handicapped persons and senior citizens, etc. all clearly reveal that righteousness is not prevalent in our society—not among individuals nor in the nation as a whole.

But in spite of that indictment against our nation, there are still some people who hunger and thirst after God and His righteousness. And the Bible assures us that God knows: "The eyes of the Lord are on the righteous, and His ears are open to their cry" (Ps. 34:15).

We can feel confident that even as evil increases among the people of our land, and all around the world, God's righteousness will continue steadfastly, for it is an attribute of His character. "God *is* righteous."

Chapter 11

GOD IS
SPIRIT

"What God is, *only* God is."

God is Spirit; *only* God is Spirit.

There are many spirit beings in existence, from the greatest (God Himself) to the lowliest. They exist on a different plane than physical beings, and have powers that we do not have, so we don't fully understand their world. But spirit beings play a crucial role in our human lives.

While each person on Earth is allowed to decide for himself whether to express good or evil in his life (through words and deeds), he lacks the generative power within himself to produce that behavior. Such generative power must be derived from a spirit source.

Behavior that is good is derived from the Spirit source of all that is good—that is, from God. Actions that are evil (i.e., contrary to God's character) are derived from the spirit source of all that is evil—that is, from Satan (whom God has allowed to be the ruler of this world for a time).

People around us can see clearly whether our allegiance is to God or to Satan, simply by observing our words and deeds, whether they be good or evil. Do we reach out in love to "others," or do we focus primarily on "self"?

When talking with the woman at the well in Samaria, Jesus made the statement, "God is Spirit" (John 4:24). Even though there was much idol worship in the region, many people believed that the true God was not a man-made idol, but living Spirit.

When Jesus said, "God is Spirit," He was not simply pointing out to the Samaritan woman that God is *a* spirit, just one among many spirit beings that exist, although it is true that God is a Spirit. Nor was Jesus suggesting that God is a spirit-force or spirit-energy, abstract and impersonal. Nor was He simply stating that God is invisible, although it's true that God is invisible (I Tim. 1:17).

His comment to the Samaritan woman was made during a discussion about worship, and Jesus was referring obliquely to the character of God— saying that God alone is worthy of worship, and "those who worship Him must worship in spirit and truth."

Because God *is* Spirit, spiritual worship is the appropriate homage to Him—the offering of the heart rather than only the lips ... the offering of the soul (mind, will, and emotion) rather than the body

30

only. We worship God, Who *is* Spirit, not only through prayer and praise, but also by living godly lives—expressing His character through words of kindness and encouragement, and through good deeds done unto others. With such worship God is well pleased.

Chapter 12

GOD IS

OMNISCIENT

"What God is, *only* God is."

God is omniscient; *only* God is omniscient.

God knows everything (I John 3:20), about everything! For example, He knows how many hairs grow on each person's head; He knows the intricacies of the human brain; He knows the complexities of nuclear physics; He knows when and where the next major earthquake will occur and how severe it will be.

God knows about events that happened in the past, and He knows what will happen in the future. How, you may ask, can He know the future? Does He control our choices and future (predestination)? No, as human beings we have freedom of choice; we determine our own fate within the parameters of our situation in life. But because God is not constrained by "time" as human beings are, He *sees* the future (like looking ahead along the time line of the physical world) and sees each choice we will make, when the time comes.

Very often our choices disappoint Him, but they don't surprise Him, for He already knows what we will do.

Confusing? It certainly is, but we are considering an omniscient (all-knowing) God with extraordinary abilities beyond our comprehension.

Because God *is* omniscient, He also knows everything about each one of us, personally—our thoughts, motives, fears, dreams, hidden agendas, etc. He knows in this personal way the millions of us who are now living, as well as all those who have lived in the past, and also each person who will live in the future. (His mind is infinite, so it's no problem for Him to handle so much information.) As the omniscient One, God knows every person through and through.

Let us consider this subject from the opposite direction: How well do we know God? We may have acquired a lot of knowledge "about God"—based on His Self-revelation through His creation, the prophets, Jesus, the Holy Spirit, visions induced by God Himself, the Bible, etc.— but how well do we actually "know God"? (There's a subtle but important difference between "knowing about" and "knowing.")

For example, if you were asked, "Do you know John Brown, the new school district superintendent?" you might answer, "Oh yes, I've been following his career for years. He's a natural leader, with innovative ideas about education."

Even if you had never met Mr. Brown personally or talked with him face to face, if you had never kept company with him, and had never enjoyed his sense of humor or been exposed to his biases, you might think you knew him ... when in reality you only knew "about him."

Very often that is the case with Christians and their knowledge of God. A believer may think he knows God, since he has attended worship services and Bible study classes for years. But if he hasn't spent much time alone with God—communicating with Him one-on-one through personal Bible reading (God speaking, with the Christian listening) and in private prayer (the Christian talking to God, as God listens)—then it's quite possible he doesn't actually "know God."

God is omniscient; *only* God is omniscient. He alone knows everything, which no one else can do ... nor should that be our desire, necessarily.

It *should* be, however, the strong desire of every believer to know God ... to understand (to the best of our ability) the desires of His heart. Knowing God in such a personal way leads to our loving Him more, and wanting to be obedient to Him ... which pleases Him very much!

36

Chapter 13

GOD IS

PURE

"What God is, ***only*** God is."

God is pure; ***only*** God is pure.

This world is a wicked place (ruled as it is by the evil one); therefore, every generation ponders the same question asked of God by the Old Testament psalmist: "How can a young person keep his way pure?" and the answer remains the same for all generations: "By guarding it according to Your word" (Ps. 119:9).

Whether we be young people or older ones, we must depend on God to direct us by His word. His word is pure (Ps. 12:6) and its purity can be relied upon—like the purification of silver subjected to the extremely high heat of a furnace, to extract the waste material and purify the metal. In like manner Christians are urged to engage in this refinement process, to "purify themselves, even as God *is* pure" (I John 3:3)—in order that they might live pure, holy, upright lives that glorify God.

In the Jewish tradition, "almost everything is purified by blood [e.g., the blood of unblemished goats and calves], and without the shedding of blood there is no forgiveness of sins" (Heb. 9:22). After many generations of animal sacrifice, God sent the Son (Jesus) to Earth to shed His blood for the forgiveness of sins of all mankind—once for all, eliminating the need for animal sacrifice. By His death and resurrection all mankind has been purified, cleansed of sin in the sight of God—a gift available to all who believe in Him.

The commandment of the Lord (i.e., that which is ordered or required by God) is pure (Ps. 19:8). It is free from any tendency to corrupt the morals or defile the soul of man, for God *is* pure.

The wisdom that is from above (i.e., from God) is first pure ... then peaceable, gentle, etc. (Jam. 3:17). The first influence of His wisdom is on the mind, to make it pure—not on the intellect, or the imagination, or the memory, or judgment, but on the *understanding*—to help man *see* what is the right thing to do. From that spirit of purity flows a righteous lifestyle, characterized by peace, gentleness, etc.

Chapter 14

GOD IS

UNCHANGING

"What God is, *only* God is."

God is unchanging; *only* God is unchanging.

Countless times as we face choices in life, we change our minds—about all manner of things: a college major, for example, or a career direction, or who to marry, or whether to live in the city or the country, or what to wear to a special family gathering, etc. Changing one's mind is normal behavior for human beings because we don't really know what the best choice is.

God, on the other hand, never changes His mind, for He is not a mortal man (I Sam. 15:29). Due to God's divine wisdom, His course of action is always correct and He doesn't need to change His mind as events unfurl. While it is true that God often regrets how things turn out for mankind, the unsatisfactory results are not His fault; they are not caused by some mistake made by God. They are the consequence of men not following God's commandments or fulfilling their obligations to God and/or others.

"I the Lord do not change," He declared (Mal. 3:6). His plans and purpose are not susceptible to change, as are those of mortal men. God has a fixed purpose (Heb. 6:17), which is as trustworthy as His unchangeable character. If He changed His plans and purpose from day to day, who could trust Him? Who could put confidence in Him?

Everything in our physical world changes with time—mountains are worn down by wind and water erosion, canyons are crafted by rushing water, the polar caps slowly melt as the Earth warms—but God remains the same (Ps. 102:27). He is a solid rock in the midst of the tempest. God does not become old and feeble-minded as time passes, nor does He become wiser or gain new powers, since He is already perfect. God *is* unchanging.

While the character of human beings can be altered by stress or shock, causing a kind-hearted person to become mean-tempered and bitter, for example, God's character never changes.

People around the world are different—in their culture, manner of dress, language, etc. The stories in the Bible record a culture much more primitive than today's technological world. But the unchanging character of God remains constant and true regardless of culture, location, or historical time frame. God is the same yesterday, today, and forever.

Thank goodness God's character is unchanging. Even as we live in this chaotic world ruled by Satan, God remains the same—unchanging and unchangeable. We can depend on Him. What a comfort.

Chapter 15

GOD IS

PATIENT

"What God is, *only* God is."

God is patient; *only* God is patient.

As the unhappy child seated in the high chair wailed and pounded his little hands on the tray, his mother turned from the kitchen sink and smiled at him fondly, saying, "Be patient, little one." We all know, of course, that being patient (i.e., waiting calmly for the desired outcome) is nearly impossible for a toddler. Even adults have difficulty being patient.

Only God—the long-suffering, constant, slow-to-anger One—*is* patient. Mankind has vexed His Spirit and tried His patience from the beginning … but still God remains patient, persevering in His hope that all men will someday love Him and keep His commandments.

God is slow-to-anger (Nahum 1:3); God is not hasty or impulsive; God is patient … but He will wait only so long. When He is provoked to anger (Ezek. 5:7ff), His furious anger eventually overcomes His patience, making it necessary for Him to impose punishment on those who show Him such utter disregard.

The Bible gives numerous examples of God's patience. When He decided to wipe out the evil from the world, God waited patiently while Noah built the Ark and gathered together the animals; and waited as Noah and his family entered the Ark; then God shut to door. God had great hopes for those eight people who survived the Flood, that they might lead future generations to walk humbly with Him. But before long He was disappointed, again.

The prophet Isaiah, in describing God's patience, said, "The Lord waits to be gracious to you" (Isa. 30:18) ... to receive their prayers of repentance and forgive their unfaithfulness, and to bless them as He had promised. But they were a stubborn people; their hearts were dark, under the influence of the prince of darkness. As punishment God brought one calamity after another upon them, hoping they would turn to Him for consolation. And repeatedly God was disappointed.

The Apostle Paul wrote of "the God of patience and consolation" (Rom. 15:5), and urged Christians "to live in harmony with one another" so that together we may glorify God.

As Christians we try to practice patience— but we can't even come close to the patience that God has demonstrated year after year and generation after generation in His dealings with mankind.

God *is* patient. Only God is perfectly patient, waiting to be gracious to us.

Chapter 16

GOD IS

SAVIOR

"What God is, *only* God is."

God is savior; *only* God is savior.

Slavery (the practice of owning other persons) has been common for thousands of years. While God undoubtedly hates the cruelty and abuse associated with slavery, He does not expressly forbid it. He set forth detailed guidelines for the Old Testament Jews regarding slavery—the acquisition, ownership, and redemption of slaves. Included in those guidelines were detailed instructions on how the freedom of a slave could be purchased for a price.

In a sense we could all be considered slaves—"slaves to sin" (John 8:34)—in *need* of a redeemer, a savior to pay the purchase price for our freedom. God is that savior, and He has already paid the price for our redemption. (It was a steep price: the death of the beloved Son on the cross).

Through the prophet Isaiah, God described Himself as "a just God and a savior" (Isa. 45:21). Those two attributes (justice and redemption) might seem like opposites, but together they accurately reflect the character of God in regard to His plan of salvation for sinful mankind. True justice would require that all mankind be condemned to eternal death, but God chose to redeem us, offering Himself as savior. The Lord Himself declared, "There is no savior besides Me" (Hosea 13:4).

The Bible tells us: "The Father sent the Son as the savior of the world" (I John 4:14), "the savior of all people" (I Tim. 4:10) who are willing to be saved by Him. Even non-Jews who heard Jesus explain God's plan of salvation (Samaritans who had come out to meet Jesus after His conversation with the woman at the well) believed and professed, "This is truly the savior of the world" (John 4:42).

Jesus purchased eternal redemption for all mankind by shedding His blood on the cross (Heb. 9:12). Because of that ultimate act of love, Jesus "is able for all time to save those who approach God through Him" (Heb 7:25).

Why would God go to such extreme measures to save mankind, when they have been such a disappointment ever since He created them? According to the psalmist, God saves sinners for His own name's sake (Ps. 106:8), for the promotion of His own glory.

Recognizing that we all need a savior, let us with grateful hearts praise God as savior; *only* God is savior.

GOD IS
PERSON

"What God is, *only* God is."

God is Person; *only* God is Person.

In stating that God *is* Person, we are also clarifying what God is not. He is not plant or animal, water, inanimate object, etc. God *is* Person. The many concepts of God or gods held by different cultures around the world vary widely—from the living Triune God worshipped by Christians to the millions of gods worshipped in India (each family having their own gods: inanimate man-made statues fashioned of wood, stone, metal, or whatever).

The Christian God is defined as Person not by psychological function (the ability to think, feel, and make choices), but rather by relational function. God is relational Person, having a relationship of love both in Himself (the three Persons in One Being) and with created beings apart from Himself.

Before going further, let us define more precisely the word "person." According to theologian Colin Gunton, there is a subtle difference in meaning between "individual" and "person": an individual is defined in terms of *separation from* other individuals, whereas a person is defined in terms of *relations with* other persons.

Because God *is* Person, He can have a relationship with other persons. He is able to hear (Exod. 2:24; 6:5) when people pray to Him—asking for help in time of trouble, giving thanks for blessings, etc.—and to respond to them. Man-made gods cannot hear or respond in any way to prayers offered up to them.

As living, loving Person, God acts in accordance with His character—He *does* what He *does* because He *is* Who He *is*. (That's the other premise put forth by theologian James A. Fowler in his article entitled "Towards a Christian Understanding of God," the deep theological treatise which prompted the writing of this "lighter" study. This second premise will be considered in a later chapter entitled "God is active.") Simply stated, God does not act in any way that is contrary to His own character of love, goodness, holiness, righteousness, etc. To do so would be to lie, to "deny Himself" (II Tim. 2:3).

God is so loving and caring and warm and personable (i.e., He is so relational!) that He draws unto Himself all those who seek peace and joy and abundant life—which He gives freely to those who love Him.

Chapter 18

GOD IS

GOD

"What God is, *only* God is."

God is God; *only* God is God.

Psychologists have said that human beings actually crave some stress and disharmony in their lives; and if problems don't present themselves naturally, people will create their own. That idea sounds outlandish to those who endure hardship in the course of their everyday lives ... those just barely keeping their heads above water in the turbulent seas swirling around them.

Would life really seem too bland and boring without problems and worries? If so, perhaps that's why so many people reject God's love and His offer of peace and protection from the evil one. Or maybe they're simply rebelling against God's requirements: "love Me and keep My commandments."

Some people choose to worship false gods who make no demands on them—gods made of stone or wood or precious metals, an image that can be fashioned by human hands and seen with the eyes. Other people worship more sophisticated, abstract gods, such as wealth, fame, and power. The Bible tells us that "those who choose another god multiply their sorrows" (Ps. 16:4).

Those who "choose another god" other than the true living God do so under the influence of Satan, "who uses all powers, signs, lying wonders, and every kind of wicked deception" to delude them so they will believe what is false. The Apostle Paul warned that all who do not love and honor God, but worship false gods instead, will be condemned (II Thes. 2:9-12) ... but obviously those who worship other gods are more concerned with this present life than with their eternal end, which Satan prefers them not to think about.

"Fools say in their hearts, 'There is no God' " (Ps. 14:1), which undoubtedly pleases Satan immensely. Those fools are an easy conquest for the evil one.

King Solomon, when seeking the very best materials with which to build the Temple in Jerusalem ("a house in which to worship God," he explained), said, "... our God is greater than other gods" (II Chron. 2:5). The psalmist David wrote: "There is none like You among the gods, O Lord ... You are great and do wondrous things; You alone are God" (Ps. 86:8-10). God Himself said it over and over to the Old Testament people: "I am the first and the last; besides Me there is no god" (Isa.

44:6); "… you shall have no other gods besides Me" (Deut. 5:7); "Is there any god besides Me? There is no other rock; I know not one" (Isa. 44:8).

But throughout the history of mankind, man has chosen to worship false gods rather than the only true God. (Satan has been very effective in his efforts to lead man astray.) God is gracious and forgiving, desiring that all men "love Him and keep His commandments," but He justly allows them freedom of choice—and His heart grieves over those who reject His love. Of course, being all-powerful, God could simply force men to love and worship Him, but that wouldn't be the same as love freely given, would it? Ultimately, His almighty power is governed by His wisdom, which He demonstrates by patiently waiting for all men to come to Him.

Those of us who love the Lord do gladly join our voices with the psalmist David as he asks, "Who is God, except the Lord?" (Ps. 18:31; also II Sam. 22:32). Let us worship the Lord, our Maker (Ps. 95:6), for He is God, and there is no other (Isa. 45:22).

God alone is God; *only* God is God.

Chapter 19

GOD IS

PEACE

"What God is, ***only*** God is."

God is peace; ***only*** God is peace.

A raging river, with turbulent brown water rushing down the watercourse, is an awesome sight ... but not one that suggests peace and serenity. A gentle, slow-moving river, on the other hand, does just that. That mood of tranquility is aptly expressed in a Christian chorus popular some years ago: "There is peace like a river in my soul" (source Isa. 48:18).

If we allow God to rule in our hearts (Col. 3:15), He will "guide our feet into the way of peace" (Luke 1:78-79). The Lord will ordain peace for us (Isa. 26:12). God *is* peace, and He blesses His people with peace (Ps. 29:11).

Long ago the Old Testament prophet Isaiah expressed these words of wisdom: "Thou wilt keep him in perfect peace whose mind is stayed on Thee" (Isa. 26:3)—and they remain true even today. A similar idea was expressed by the Apostle Paul in his letter to the Christians at Rome: "... be transformed by the renewing of your minds" (12:2). If we sincerely desire that God fill our minds and hearts with His character, and if we open ourselves unreservedly to His indwelling, He will give us peace (II Thes. 3:16). "The effect of righteousness will be peace" (Isa. 32:17).

But for the wicked there is no peace, says God (Isa. 48:22; 57:21). They may enjoy temporary peace and prosperity, but there is no abiding peace ... for "the wicked are like the troubled sea ... whose waters cast up mire and dirt" (Isa. 57:20). The waters of the sea may appear to be calm at times, but they are never entirely calm; they are always in motion ... and occasionally they are whipped into waves that roll and foam and dash upon the shore. Such is the unsettling turmoil in the heart of wicked men.

Before the Son was sent to Earth, Isaiah prophesied about the child that was to come, saying that one of the names by which He would be known was Prince of Peace (Isa. 9:6). His indwelling Spirit in Christians allows them to experience "peace that passes all understanding" (Phlp. 4:7)..

God's peace will shield us from the distressing anxiety caused by trials and tribulations of this world, if we but ask Him. Of course God knows already what difficulties we face, without our bringing them to His attention—but He desires that we come to Him, to cast all our cares upon Him, to spread our concerns out before Him … for it is by this act of prayer and supplication that the close emotional connection is maintained between God and His children.

Only in God, Who *is* peace, can our minds and hearts be kept in peace.

Chapter 20

GOD IS
OMNIPOTENT

"What God is, *only* God is."

God is omnipotent; *only* God is omnipotent.

To Abraham God declared, "I am God Almighty" (Gen. 17:1)—the all-powerful One, omnipotent. God told Abraham (age 99) that his wife Sarah (age 90) would soon bear him a son, to be named Isaac. Abraham laughed at the absurdity of the idea, but it happened just as the Lord said it would.

The Bible says that the Almighty God occasionally spoke directly to men. He talked with Adam in the Garden of Eden; He spoke to Noah about building the Ark; He spoke to Abraham about giving him a son Isaac and many descendants; He spoke to Moses about leading those descendants out of slavery in Egypt to the Promised Land; He spoke to the prophet Ezekiel about delivering the Jewish people from Captivity, etc.

When the Almighty God speaks, His voice is powerful (Ps. 29:4). It is sometimes described as the sound of rushing water or wind, or as thunder (Job 40:9)—but somehow it's still understandable.

The Apostle Paul refers to God's "eternal power" (Rom. 1:20), noting that it is clearly seen through the things He made.

God's power is always in force, even at times when it doesn't appear evident; for example, on the night Jesus was betrayed and arrested in the Garden of Gethsemane under cover of darkness. When taken before the Jewish high priest for questioning, Jesus referred to God by the title "power," saying, "Hereafter you shall see the Son of man sitting on the right hand of power" (Matt. 26:64; Mark 14:62; Luke 22:69). Jesus had no doubt of God's power and control of all things, even as He faced His own physical death on Earth.

Today, under Satan's rule, chaos and disorder prevail on Earth … but one day the Almighty God will exert His power by taking control away from the evil one and setting up His divine kingdom over all the world (Rev. 11:17). The Lord will reign supreme and will be honored everywhere on Earth, as He is in Heaven.

When that time comes, do you suppose some enterprising saint will be distributing T-shirts with the logo "God rules!" printed on them? And will God give a wry smile and a nod of approval? He just might.

Chapter 21

GOD IS

TRUTH

"What God is, *only* God is."

God is truth; *only* God is truth.

In a courtroom setting a witness called to testify
before the court is asked, "Will you tell the truth,
the whole truth, and nothing but the truth?"—to
which an affirmative response is required before the
witness can begin his testimony. To lie after taking
such an oath is punishable under the law. Lying is
both a legal offense and a moral one.

It is sometimes difficult, however, to
determine "What is truth?" ... for error often seems
plausible: it may seem to promote virtue and
happiness, to promote religion, etc. But in reality,
no lie or error or falsehood has its origin in the truth
(I John 2:21). To determine "what is truth," we
need a standard of truth for comparison. There is
no better standard than God ... for God *is* truth.

The Old Testament psalmist declared, "The
sum of Thy word is truth" (Ps. 119:160), a concept
expressed also by Jesus in prayer to the Father:

"Thy word is truth" (John 17:17)—the word "truth" meaning: honesty, accuracy, seeing things as they really are, free from error or falsehood. God's word (His teaching, His commandments) is based on His own character, on His own attributes of love and truth (Ps. 25:10), which manifest all that God *is* and *does*.

Since God *is* truth, He never lies (Titus 1:2); for to do so would be to deny Himself (II Tim. 2:13), to deny His own nature. God never acts in a manner contrary to His own character.

Jesus referred to Himself as the truth ("I am the way, the truth, and the life"—John 14:6) and referred to the Holy Spirit as "the Spirit of truth" (John 14:17, 15:26). Jesus, Who was "full of grace and truth" (John 1:14), represented the reality of things ... for the Triune God—the Father, Jesus the Son, and the Holy Spirit—*is* truth.

Sometimes a Christian feels compelled to "speak the truth" to another believer, to point out to him the error of his ways. That Christian should proceed with caution, for Satan is skilled at using such judgmental words (usually expressed under the guise of sincere "Christian concern") to offend and cause discord within the group of believers. The Bible warns, "Judge not, lest you be judged," and advises the accuser to first remove the beam from his own eye before pointing out the speck in his brother's eye (Matt. 7:1-5).

If the accuser, after spending time in sincere private prayer to examine his own motives, still feels compelled to speak out—believing it is his genuine desire to help the other person see the truth, turn away from error, and walk more humbly with God—only then should the accuser proceed to "speak the truth" … with gentleness and kindness and, most definitely, in private. To speak of the matter in the presence of others clearly reveals that the accuser's intent is not to help the accused person, but rather to publicly humiliate and shame him. Such behavior is most assuredly generated by the deceiver, not by God.

Always, Christians should "speak the truth *in love*" (Eph. 4:15) … to build up, to encourage, to strengthen— never to put down. That simple phrase—"in love"—should be the keystone of all our words and deeds in our relations with other people, just as it is with God in His dealings with mankind.

God always speaks the truth "in love," for God is truth; *only* God is truth.

Chapter 22

GOD IS

WISE

"What God is, *only* God is."

God is wise; *only* God is wise.

In civilized nations, where much emphasis is placed on **knowledge**, the children are taught from a young age such abstract concepts as letters, numbers, time, and space. As the children mature and continue to study, they gain **understanding** (seeing the meaning or importance of the knowledge they have acquired). A small percentage of them continue learning into adulthood, in search of **wisdom**.

Men seek wisdom to find the underlying reason—the "why"—of things they have learned through investigation or personal experience. But wisdom cannot be acquired simply through study; it is the Lord Who gives wisdom to men.

The Lord gives wisdom (Prov. 2:6) to those who ask for it. King David recognized that only God could impart wisdom, and he asked for it: "teach me wisdom" (Ps. 51:6). King Solomon also asked for wisdom, and the Lord gave him very great wisdom (I Kings 4:29). At the request of the prophet Ezra, God gave him wisdom to appoint judges (Ezra 7:25). "If any of you is lacking in wisdom," wrote James to new Christians, "ask God … and it will be given you" (1:5).

Wisdom in its fullness/completeness is found only in God. God is wise; *only* God is wise.

When Satan, in the guise of a serpent in the Garden of Eden, told Eve that eating fruit from the tree of the knowledge of good and evil would make her "like God," she was enticed to eat, thinking it would make her wise like God (Gen. 3:6). That act of disobedience opened the eyes of Adam and Eve, but it did not make them wise like God; it did, however, get them kicked out of the Garden. (Undoubtedly God gave a deep sigh of disappointment as they were escorted out.)

The psalmist declared, "The fear of the Lord is the beginning of wisdom" (Ps. 111:10); i.e., reverence for the Lord is the very foundation of wisdom. Only God is perfectly wise (I Tim. 1:17). He is wise in heart (Job 9:4), and His wisdom is pure, peaceable, gentle (James 3:13-17). At the same time, wisdom and strength are His (Job 12:13); His power is governed by His wisdom.

The wisdom of God is described as "rich variety" (Eph. 3:10) … think diversified, like the variegated hues of pink and gold and lavender in the sky when the lowering sun is reflected off the clouds at sunset. Truly, God is amazing! Not only is the wisdom of God profound, it is also beautiful! God is wise; *only* God is wise.

Chapter 23

GOD IS

ACTIVE

"What God is, *only* God is."

God is active; *only* God is active.

What does God do all day? According to the Bible He never sleeps (Ps. 121:3-4); nor is He passive, simply observing all that is happening on Earth and in the heavens. God is *always* active, never needing rest. Only God can be active in that way, for "what God is, *only* God is."

He keeps watch on the evil and the good (Prov. 15:3). He hears and answers the prayers of those who call upon Him (Ps. 34:4). He strengthens those whose heart is true to Him (II Chron. 16:9); He satisfies the thirsty and fills the hungry (Ps. 107:9).

God *is* active, at all times, doing what only He can do because of Who/what He is. His actions are a manifestation (a demonstration, a revelation) of His own character ... or, as stated by Christian theologian James A. Fowler, "God *does* what He *does* because He *is* Who He *is*." God's actions are always consistent with His character; He never acts "out of character"; He never acts contrary to Who/what He is.

Let us consider a few of examples:

Because God *is* faithful, He protected the Israelites as they fled from Egypt. He parted the waters of the Red Sea (He even dried the ground! — Ps. 66:6) so the Israelites could cross over safely before He released the waters to drown the Egyptian soldiers who were in pursuit.

Because God *is* good, He provided for the needs of the Israelites during the 40 years they wandered in the desert (the wandering was God's just punishment for their failure to trust Him) ... and then He led them safely back to the Promised Land.

Because God *is* love, He reproves and disciplines those whom He loves (Rev. 3:19). Even when God punished the Israelites for worshipping idols, He did so out of love, hoping they would see the error of their ways and turn to Him for consolation.

And because God *is* love, He sent the beloved Son to Earth to die for all mankind. Love in action!

God *does* what He *does* because He *is* Who He *is*. God *is* active, always active. He expresses His divine character through His actions. That's what God does all day, and all night, unceasingly.

Chapter 24

GOD IS
FAITHFUL

"What God is, *only* God is."

God is faithful; *only* God is faithful.

When God explained details of the Ten Commandments to Moses, He emphasized that He would remain faithful and keep His covenant promises to the "chosen people" even to the thousandth generation—as they loved Him and kept His commandments. But the people didn't love God enough to keep His commandments ... so He punished them with drought and hardship, military defeat, exile from the Promised Land, etc.—all in the hope that they would turn to Him, love Him, and keep His commandments.

They were unfaithful to God, but in spite of their unfaithfulness, He was faithful to them, just as He promised. He did not stop loving them or be false to His faithfulness.

What God said all those many years ago still holds true today, for all peoples and nations. No matter what happens, and how disappointing mankind is to God, He still remains faithful (true to His word, loyal, worthy of trust).

Some people may claim to be loyal, dependable, faithful—but among human beings "who can find one who is faithful?" (Prov. 20:6).

As Christians we cling to God's promise that He will always be faithful. The Bible says that "the Lord is faithful; He will strengthen you and guard you from the evil one" (II Thes. 3:3). It assures us that "God is faithful, and He will not let you be tested beyond your strength" (I Cor. 10:13). (If the Old Testament story of Job comes to mind, we can only pray that God will never test us to that degree.)

God is faithful; *only* God is faithful. Without doubt, we can place our full trust in His faithfulness, both for life now and life after death

Chapter 25

GOD IS
SOVEREIGN

"What God is, *only* God is."

God is sovereign; *only* God is sovereign.

The Lord our God is King of kings and Lord of
lords
(I Tim. 6:15). He *is* sovereign, having supreme
rank, authority, and power over all the kingdoms of
mortal men (Dan. 4:17).

God's sovereignty is everlasting, throughout
eternity. While human kings die and cannot exert
their authority over the generations to follow (Dan.
4:34), the sovereign God continues on as King of
the ages (I Tim. 1:17), the divine Ruler over all the
kingdoms of the earth (Ps. 103:19).

Sometimes the ruling monarch of an earthly
kingdom is a fair and just authority over the people,
but very often that isn't the case. As a common
adage states, "Power corrupts, and absolute power
corrupts absolutely." Even so, men are to accept
the authority of those in power over them (I Pet.
2:13), for it is God Who places kings in their

positions of authority, for His own purposes. "He deposes kings and sets up kings" (Dan. 2:21).

One day Jesus was put to the test regarding allegiance to governing powers. The Pharisees sent their disciples to Him to ask, "Is it right to pay taxes to Caesar?" Jesus, aware of the malice in their hearts, asked to see the coin used to pay the tax. They showed Him, and on it was imprinted the head of Caesar. Then Jesus answered, "Give to Caesar the things that are Caesar's, and to God the things that are God's" (Matt. 22:15-22). Those questioning Him went away amazed at His wisdom.

God reigns supreme both on Earth and in Heaven. The psalmist David asked, "Who is the King of glory?" and answered, "The Lord, strong and mighty" (Ps. 24:8). He repeated the question (in vs. 10) and answered, "The Lord of hosts" (referring to the angels which surround the throne of God)—where "the Lord sits enthroned as King forever"
(Ps. 29:10).

God is sovereign (Ruler over all); *only* God is sovereign.

Chapter 26

GOD IS

ETERNAL

"What God is, *only* God is."

God is eternal; *only* God is eternal.

The word "eternal" is defined as: without beginning or end. Only God *is* eternal. He has no beginning; He alone has always existed—the Self-existent One. And because God is also immortal (exempt from death), He will never die; He will have no end. "The Lord exists forever" (Ps. 119:89).

"Eternal life" is a term infrequently found in the Old Testament writings, but it was a concept well known to the Jews of that time. Jesus spoke often of eternal life during His brief earthly ministry. To the Jews, Jesus said, "You search the scriptures because in them you think you have eternal life. The scriptures testify about Me, yet you refuse to come to Me to have life" (John 5:39).

Jesus described Himself as "the One Who descended from Heaven, the Son of Man," and went on to say that the Son of Man must be lifted up (on the cross of crucifixion) so that whoever believes in Him may have eternal life (John 3:13-15).

Just as the Apostle Paul admonished young Timothy to "shun evil; pursue righteousness, godliness, faith, love, endurance, gentleness. ... take hold of the eternal life to which you were called" (I Tim. 6:11-12), we should do the same, to "take hold of the eternal life" God has promised to all who believe in Him (I John 2:25).

While we usually think of eternal life as something to be inherited after death and enjoyed in Heaven (and indeed, it is!), in a sense we already experience eternal life here on Earth, as God abides in us and we in Him. But at the same time, we long for Heaven, where we will see Him face to face and enjoy His eternal glory, to which He has called us (I Pet. 6:10). That will be the ultimate joy: abiding with the eternal God in His heavenly kingdom forevermore.

Chapter 27

GOD IS

JOY

"What God is, *only* God is."

God is joy; *only* God is joy.

The indwelling Holy Spirit produces fruit (i.e., virtue/
godliness) in the lives of Christians (Gal. 5:22). That fruit includes love, joy, peace, patience, etc. Note how precisely the list of fruit echoes the character of God.

God *is* joy. Not just momentary happiness, but deep abiding joy, complete joy. As that divine attribute of joy is reproduced in Christians by the indwelling Spirit, we are given strength to meet the challenges of life. The Old Testament prophet Nehemiah proclaimed, "The joy of the Lord is your strength" (Neh. 8:10) ... strength to live in this world among men who practice evil.

The psalmist David wrote, "In Your presence there is fullness of joy" (Ps. 16:11). The phrase "fullness of joy" suggests there is more than the joy intermingled with sorrow that we experience in this world. In God's presence in Heaven will be found a totally satisfying, unclouded joy without end. While there is a hint of that future "fullness of joy" in our communion with God in prayer, and in the sense of peace that surrounds us as we "love Him and keep His commandments," that perfect fullness of joy resides in Heaven. Even the angels in Heaven share in it, for there is much joy among the angels in Heaven over every sinner who repents and turns to God (Luke 15:10).

God gives joy to those who please Him, to those who are good/righteous in His sight (Ec. 2:26). King David, after sinning by going in to Bathsheba, felt the absence of that joy ... and having repented of his sin, David pleaded with God: "Restore to me the joy of Your salvation" (Ps. 51:12). Is it not the same with us? ... that sin strips away the joy; we lose peace of mind; we feel separated from God?

Fortunately, God is always ready to forgive and welcome us back into His joy.

Chapter 28

GOD IS
OMNIPRESENT

*"What God is, **only** God is."*

God is omnipresent; **only** God is omnipresent.

How can any human being rightly comprehend the omnipresent nature of God? As the omnipresent One, He is present in all places, everywhere, all at the same time, at every moment. Only the true God, Who can do all things, could possibly be omnipresent.

Mankind, created by God as physical beings, can be in only one place at a time. But the Lord our God, a boundless Spirit unconstrained by the limitations of space and time, is everywhere, all at the same time!

In Old Testament days God revealed His omnipresent nature to the prophets, who found it as amazing then as we do today. To Isaiah He said, I dwell in Heaven and also on Earth with the contrite and humble of spirit (Isa. 57:15). The psalmist David included the truth of God's remarkable omnipresence in a psalm: If I ascend to the heavens, You are there; if I make my bed in Sheol,

You are there; if I take the wings of the morning to the farthest limits of the sea, You are there (Ps. 139:7-10).

When God was leading Moses and the "chosen people" to the Promised Land, He assured Moses that His presence would go with them (Exod. 33:14). Years later, when the people continually provoked God to anger by not keeping His commandments, He Himself overcame their enemies; it was "His presence that saved them" (Isa. 63:5-9).

When the prophet Jonah didn't want to go to Ninevah as God directed him, he tried to flee from His presence ... to no avail. God was present with Jonah as he boarded the ship headed in the opposite direction, and He was still with him when he sat weeping and repenting in the stomach of the whale (Jonah 1:3-10). And of course He accompanied Jonah to Ninevah where he accomplished God's Will.

Because God *is* omnipresent, wherever we happen to be, at any time, we are in the presence of God. To those of us who love Him, His omnipresence is a comforting thought, for it means we can never accidentally stray out of His presence. Even when we cannot sense His presence, He is with us. Sometimes we may seek Him but cannot find Him, as did Job during his season of testing— "If I go forward, He is not there; or backward ... or to the left ... or the right, I cannot behold Him" (Job 23:8-9)—but God is there, always.

Rejoice, you who love the Lord, for God *is* omnipresent. *Only* God is omnipresent.

Chapter 29

GOD IS

PERFECT

"What God is, *only* God is."

God is perfect; *only* God is perfect.

Some years ago (in the mid-20th century) there was a whimsical song written about kids. The lyrics included these lines: "Why can't they be like we were? *Perfect* in every way! What's the matter with kids today?" That reference to being perfect was made tongue-in-cheek, of course, since no one is perfect ... except God (Matt. 5:48).

Jesus, when seated on a hillside speaking to a large group of people, declared that God *is* perfect, and He urged those in the crowd to be perfect. He didn't mean they could *be* perfect "like God"—blameless, sinless, lacking nothing— but that they should try to exhibit God's perfection in their attitudes and actions.

The Bible tells us that God's way is perfect (II Sam. 22:31; Ps. 18:30). That is to say, God's doings, His actions, are without fault, complete.

God is perfect in knowledge; He knows all things. The wondrous works of the One Who can command the lightning and hold the clouds suspended in the air demonstrate this truth (Job 37:16). Job was described as a perfect and upright man (Job 1:1,8), but he was not sinless—not perfect "like God." He was a devout, moral, and ethical man, and God was pleased with him.

The law of the Lord is perfect (Ps. 19:7), declared the psalmist David. He was referring to God's instruction or teaching given through the Law; it is complete as a revelation of truth, it is complete as a rule of conduct.

The writer of the letter to the Hebrews prayed that God would make those early Christians perfect in every good work to do His Will (Heb. 13:20-21), asking God to provide whatever strength/wisdom was needed for them to remain faithful.

The Apostle James wrote a letter of encouragement urging Christians to rejoice in trials and tribulations, which produce patience (James 1:3) ... which in turn produces strength of character (perfect work or important effects on the soul)— "that you may be perfect and complete," lacking in nothing that would perfect/complete your character.

While we strive to be perfect and complete like God, we know that we cannot attain that goal. Only God *is* perfect. "There is none like God" (Deut. 33:26).

God is perfect in every way! He is desirous of expressing His perfect character in those who are receptive to Him by faith.

Chapter 30

GOD IS

INFINITE

"What God is, *only* God is."

God is infinite; *only* God is infinite.

Infinity is difficult for human minds to grasp. It is defined as: something that goes on and on, without end, beyond measure. Our finite minds struggle to understand such a concept. Even so, we are introduced to the idea at a young age, usually as pre-teen math students told to imagine a number line extending out into the beyond—the numbers getting larger and larger, one by one, without end.

Another example of infinity is the vastness of outer space—the heavens created by God. Who knows how many universes and galaxies exist out there, beyond our sight? (Well, actually, God knows, because He created it all.)

God is infinite; *only* God is infinite. Everything about Him is infinite, unlimited, boundless. The Bible tells of God's infinite nature. His very existence is infinite; it has no end (Ps. 102:27). His understanding is infinite (Ps. 147:5).

His reign as Prince of Peace over all Heaven and Earth shall be unlimited; i.e., a reign of unlimited peace (Isa. 9:7). God's mind is infinite; therefore His creativity, His imagination, His memory (His ability to process and store for later retrieval an unlimited amount of information, etc.) is unlimited.

God *is* infinite, in all ways. Those of us who love Him strive to be "like Him"—in fact, the Bible exhorts us to do so: to be holy as God is holy, and righteous as God is righteous, and good as God is good, etc.—but that goal can never be fully achieved by human beings ... no matter how earnestly we pray:

> O to be like Thee, O to be like Thee,
> Blessed Redeemer, pure as Thou art.
> Come in Thy sweetness, come in Thy
>   fullness,
> Stamp Thine own image deep on my heart.
>
> (Chorus of beloved Christian hymn entitled "O to Be Like Thee")

Perhaps this is the attribute of God that most clearly defines *why* we can never be "like God." God *is* infinite, without limitations of any kind ... while man is but a limited, finite being—made in the image of God, but not infinite "like God."

We can praise God for being such an awesome God, and we can love Him and keep His commandments to the best of our ability (which pleases Him immensely) … but we can never be "like God." We are finite beings, while God is infinite; *only* God is infinite.

Chapter 31

GOD IS

JUDGE

"What God is, *only* God is."

God is judge; *only* God is judge.

Christians are warned not to "pass judgment on one another" (Rom. 14:13). "Judge not, lest you be judged. You will be judged in like measure" (Matt. 7:1-2), explained Jesus. When we need to make judgments, we should follow God's directive: "render judgments that are true and *make for peace*" (Zech. 8:16).

In Heaven God has prepared His throne for judgment (Ps. 9:7-8), where the eternal fate of each person will be decided. Jesus said that He was given authority by the Father to execute judgment (John 5:27-30), and then He clarified that by saying, "It is not I alone Who judge, but I and the Father Who sent Me" (John 8:16) ... recalling to mind the radical statement He made in the Temple one day: "I and the Father are one."

Each of us, at the appointed time, must appear before the judgment seat of God (Rom.

14:10). God, through Jesus, will judge our secret thoughts (Rom. 2:16) as well as our words and deeds, both righteous and wicked. On that day, as we give an account of our lives to God, He will be looking upon our hearts, which clearly reveal the true answer to His ultimate question: "Do you love Me?"

According to Matthew's gospel record (25:32-46), Jesus declared that at the time of judgment all the nations will be gathered before the throne, and the Son will separate the people one from another, putting the sheep at His right and the goats at the left.

To those at His right hand (the sheep) He will say, "Come inherit the kingdom prepared for you from the foundation of the world ... for you gave Me food and drink when I was hungry and thirsty, you clothed Me when I was naked, you cared for Me when I was sick, you visited Me in prison. ... When you did these things unto the least of these, you did them unto Me." And to those at His left (the goats) He will say, "Depart from Me into the eternal fire prepared for the devil and his angels ... for you did not care for those among you who were hungry and thirsty, and naked, and sick, and in prison. ... As you did unto them, you did unto Me."

God is judge of all mankind; *only* God is judge. He will judge with righteousness, according to His nature. Even though not everyone will be

welcomed into God's heavenly kingdom, the Bible declares that His judgment of all the world will be a time of rejoicing: the heavens shall be glad, the earth shall rejoice, the sea shall roar, the field shall exult, the trees of the forest shall sing for joy before the Lord
(I Chron. 16:31-33).

May we be among those who *are* welcomed into God's heavenly kingdom. Our desire is expressed so joyfully in this chorus:

> When we all get to Heaven,
> What a day of rejoicing that will be!
> When we all see Jesus,
> We'll sing and shout the victory!

* * * * *

Hymns Quoted

Holy, Holy, Holy!
>*Words by:* Reginald Heber, 1826
>*Music by:* John B. Dykes, 1861

O to Be Like Thee!
>*Words by:* Thomas O. Chisholm, 1897
>*Music by:* William J. Kirkpatrick, 1897

When We All Get to Heaven
>*Words by:* Eliza E. Hewitt, 1898
>*Music by:* Emily D. Wilson, 1898

Additional copies of this book can be
purchased from select Christian bookstores

-or-

ordered on-line from
www.Amazon.com

Thank you!

www.ingramcontent.com/pod-product-compliance
Lightning Source LLC
Chambersburg PA
CBHW060039040426
42331CB00032B/1547